Hot Chocolate

Andrea Almada
Illustrated by Monique Passicot

A Harcourt Achieve Imprint

www.Rigby.com
1-800-531-5015

This is
Grandma's house.

We like to go
to Grandma's house.

It is cold today.
We make a hot drink.
We all help.

We make it with milk.

Dora gets the cups.
Carlos gets the spoons.

6

"I will get the bar of chocolate," said Omar.

Grandma puts the milk in the pot.
The milk gets very hot.

"Hot milk and chocolate
make nice
hot chocolate,"
said Grandma.

Grandma said,
"Stay away
from the pot.
The milk is too hot."

We stay away.

Then Grandma said,
"Now we have
hot chocolate!
Get your cups!"

Grandma fills the cups.

We all like Grandma's hot chocolate.

It is so good!